The Soldiers of Year II

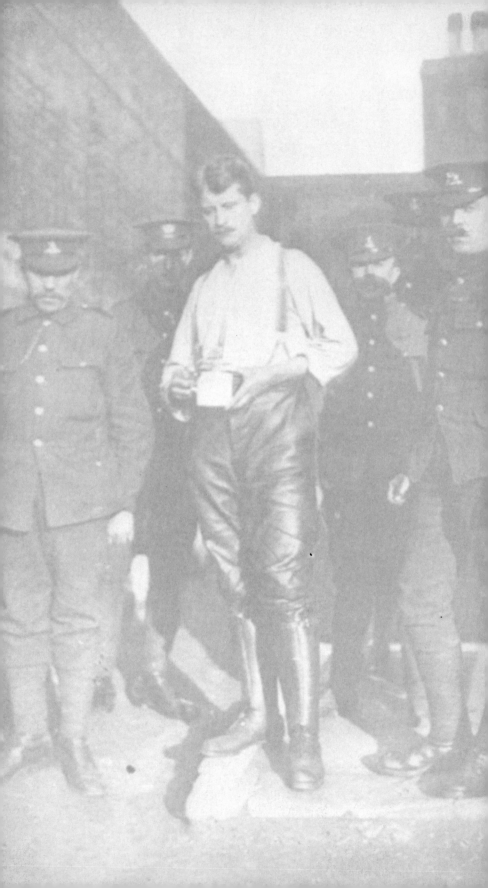

Medbh McGuckian

The Soldiers
of
Year II

with an Afterword by Guinn Batten

WAKE FOREST UNIVERSITY PRESS

Wake Forest University Press
This book is for sale only in
North America.
Copyright © Medbh McGuckian
First U.S. Edition published 2002
All rights reserved. For permis-
sion, required to reproduce
or broadcast more than several
lines, write to:
Wake Forest University Press
Post Office Box 7333, Winston-
Salem, NC 27109.
Printed in the United States of
America by Thomson-Shore.
Text set in Minion and Trinité.
Book designed by R. Eckersley.
Afterword © Guinn Batten
The editors wish to thank Sheila
Ewing for editorial assistance.
Many of these poems, in a differ-
ent selection and arrangement,
were published in *Drawing
Ballerinas* (2001) and *The Face
of the Earth* (2002) by The Gallery
Press, Co. Meath, Ireland.
Library of Congress Catalogue
Card Number: 2002106022
ISBN (paperback) 1-930630-08-5
ISBN (cloth) 1-930630-09-3

To Gregory and Véronique

Contents

THE PALACE OF TODAY

13 Helen's War

15 The Palace of Today

17 Speranza

18 Life as a Literary Convict

20 Revival of Gathered Scents

22 Love Affair with Firearms

23 Birthday Composition of Horses

24 The Chimney Boys

26 Filming the Famine

28 Turning the Sleep Spindle

29 Blood-Words

30 The Walking of the Land

32 Operation Market Garden

34 Ring Size M½

35 Antebellum Backlash

36 The Fissure of Sylvius

37 The Modern Proserpine

39 The Half-Marriage

40 To Such a Hermes

41 Blue Kasina

43 The Language Renters

44 Black Magnificat

46 Soliloquy to a Cloud

48 To Make Two Bridges Necessary

49 The Muse Hater's Small Green Passion

51 Round Square

52 The Soldiers of Year II

53 Safe House

54 The Starling House

55 Lorica

56 Mating with the Well

57 An Invalid in War

58 Thinking of the Whole Island

59 *Idée Mère*

60 A Poem for St. Patrick's Day

61 Love-Spot

63 Nightingale-Nights

65 A Religion of Writing

66 Clara Theme

68 Pincushion with Beaded Cross

70 English as a Foreign Language

72 Hessian, Linen, Silk

73 Photocall

74 The Gregory Quarter-Acre Clause

75 Thunder: Perfect Mind

76 Gander Month

77 Fourteenth Century Hours of the Virgin

78 Our Lady's Bedstraw

79 Making Your Own Eclipse

82 This Ember Week

84 The Change Worshipper

86 The Fortified Song of Flowers

87 To My Disordered Muse

89 Three Rings, Six Graves

from *Drawing Ballerinas*

93 At Mullaghmore

94 Drawing Ballerinas

96 A Ballet Called 'Culloden'

97 The Mickey-Mouse Gas Mask

98 The Orange Island

99 Butcher's Table

100 The Frost Fair

101 The Colony Room

102 Condition Three

104 Angelus Bells and the Light Glinting in Her Hair

105 The Swan Trap

106 A Perfume Called 'My Own'

107 A Mantra of Submission

108 The Miniver

109 The Flora of Mercury

111 Moonflowers

113 *Gaeltacht na Fuiseoige*

114 Red Trial

116 Hazel Lavery, The Green Coat, 1926

118 Black Raven on Cream-Coloured Background

120 Monody for Aghas

122 Oration

125 Afterword

The Palace of Today

Helen's War

Bertie finished early. He was nineteen when he returned from the training college at Strawberry Hill. There was a job going in the local school in Glenshesk, and you'd think they would have given it to him, eldest of twelve children, parents lifetime parishioners, but no, Pat Duffin got it and your father I'm sure was brighter than him. But that's the way of the world and it didn't do him much good in the end, for he died within a few years of T.B. All Bertie could get was subbing jobs, in Loughgiel and Magherahoney – Mrs. McCollum that just died across the road, her uncle was the principal. They were very fond of him in Magherahoney.

Then there was one Sunday Bertie and I were at Mass, and just putting our pennies on the plate, and the priest asked how he was doing, and Bertie was able to say to him, he'd just been offered a permanent post in Belfast. He didn't know how to take this, and I couldn't help adding: 'I don't see why you couldn't have given him the job here, father, and saved him going all that way from home.' It was shortly after that I took sick, and maybe it had something to do with talking back to a priest. I was only twenty three then, and was on my back for three years.

Bertie went to the city for the first time on October 1st, 1942. The Thursday before he died he was up here, and in good form, except at one point he looked serious and commented: 'It's fifty years ago to the day, Helen, that I first set foot in Belfast.' He had bad digs, most of the time, though one woman he stayed with was from Ballycastle, and treated him well. He had a violin left to him, and it disappeared somehow with all the moves. On July 6th, 1943, I was brought to Foster Green Hospital in Belfast by taxi. We went out for a drink before I left but I wasn't able for it. They put you over while they inserted a tube to draw the fluid off the lungs, and you had to lie completely flat with it, or it came out; and once it came out with me, and they didn't put me over putting it back in again, only brandy and that, I'll never forget it, so I swore I wouldn't move again, and I didn't for three years.

Bertie was evacuated to Saul in County Down with the school-children, but he still visited every Sunday and often during the week as well. He had different girls but he never brought your mother up. There were people dying all the time round me but I wouldn't die *for* them. It wasn't that I was strong, I just had this will to live. Then they took me to the Royal to do the operation, and Bertie gave blood for it. I have no ribs on this side, they took them all away to cut the lung out, or most of it. But there was still fluid in what remained. We got St. Anne's ointment and Lourdes water, but there was no penicillin available for they needed it all for the soldiers. Then one day in 1946 they brought in this wee bottle of stuff over from England that cost about £800, and the next week I was able to go home.

You know how when you've got used to a place, or institutionalised, you don't want to leave. Bertie came with me on the train, and I didn't know where I was, I couldn't make anything out, everything was strange to me. They were all there except Margaret, and that spoiled the day for me, for she was already ill, and died the following March in the big snow.

Your mother didn't bring you up much on account of it. Once I wanted to take you down the lane to the haunted house, the fairies' house, we would have had a great day, but she wouldn't let me take you through the grass in case you got your feet wet. We were just setting off, when she gave this cry, or shriek, from the gate, and so we had to turn back.

The Palace of Today

I.M. OSCAR WILDE

The meaning is very much
a rhythmical one, the same law
in blossom on the shoulder-high
fork of a shrub-like tree,
just streaming out presence
and expecting nothing.

The pew resembles a half-open
tomb or a sort of kennel
for gazing out of themselves,
their lives overgrown like an old path,
turning into their opposite,
when they let the handkerchief fall.

The slowness of his tread
seems to call for no great effort,
it revolves only thirty times a minute.
Because the treads are set so
very far apart, he has to stretch
his limbs to their utmost

in order to reach the step.
So that one of his legs is always
in mid-air, and takes the whole
of his weight when it lands.
During this his body remains
completely motionless,

the slowness of the movement
is enough to make his head spin
and strain the muscles of his stomach.
Sometimes he loses consciousness
and falls from the top of the wheel.
I watched men and children

as they came off, and not one
had the slightest trace of sweat,
on the contrary, all appeared
to be cold, all pale, almost blue,
like the sage-brush branch our carriage
caught, near steps of unpeeled log.

Speranza

There is a war now to be fought
in her two-armed form: a cold
current only hours old
in her honeylike blood.

Spring reaches deep into her chest wall,
a deep, old, empty need
with no unspoken lines
and no words that are the wrong ones.

Lung pictures, white mould on leaves,
fractions of heart, the simpler bacteria
of meaning, slow her breath
to the tenderest of religions,

while a pale leafing voice,
burned clean, not yet awake from winter,
breathes her likely death into
my midnight-starved mouth.

Life as a Literary Convict

I have experienced a wilderness
printed black on white.
Tarnished years of silver fever.
All my minds are weapons.

I miss the tunic of rain that settled in
like an old heart complaint,
the polluted air so bracing,
the great non-meetings
wrapped up in politics.

Signs of the still recent war
creep among the people like a plague,
dressed as Phoebus.
While I wander about in search of the dead,
all I see are the living,
being pulled into full existence,
emerging as if from a cellar.

Everything that ended in gunshots
and news of massacres
and third-class funerals that smelled
of nothing, pressed out of my reader's eye
the last tears of childhood.

Ceilings were lowered and gardens
obliterated, the deaf and the absent-
minded were being shot,
but the clockwork life of the unchanging
street, and the uninterrupted houses in rows
neutralised the lava of war
to a normal part of winter
at an enormous cost.

Fresh families pose like birds
in the wound-up spring, healing
at a distance in a slower time.
The roughneck soldier that fell
in a flooded field has managed to create
a republic without republicans.

He lies in his English envelope
like the Greek word for Greekness,
defender of Throne and Altar,
while the frontier is guarded
by the small wombs of two chickens.

Revival of Gathered Scents

Someone will tap a door
with just a single finger,
while beaks are still tucked under wings,

and the woman nestling
close to the blinds
has received a letter in the dark:

a knotted letter, snow-moistened,
the ink-seal on the outside frozen.
She tries to unfasten the rice-paste,

her sleep-swollen eyes aching
at the ink extremely dark
in some places, light in others.

The paper white as a flower
wraps up a single petal of mountain rose,
whose dead white head remains

alone in the fields. It cannot
withstand the autumn's strength
with a cheap prayer,

expecting too many years.
The house is one where no one
cares about the gate,

and for a time the pond
stays as it was, the entire garden
is the same green colour,

and the two stars seem
closer than usual, fern on the tiles.
Now she has carefully scented a robe

of glossed silk, beaten and stretched,
with a pattern of decaying wood
and chrysanthemums faded in part

at the hems; yet she seems
perfectly clad, high-kneeling
to the God of Leaves

at the small half-shutters,
at the very edge of roofs.
Because the tree pear-skinned,

streaked with rain,
is divided into a thousand branches
full of curved promises

whose leaves do not change.
How depressing when there is
no reply poem, no return poem

written on a fan with three
ribs! No next morning letter
attached to a spray of clover

with a long iris root enclosed,
clear-toned as the face a child
has drawn on a melon.

Love Affair with Firearms

From behind the moon boys' graves
bleed endlessly; from photograph
to browning photograph they blacken
headlines, stranded outside of time
at the story's frigid edge.

Though they are long buried
in French soil, we are still speaking
of trenches, of who rose, who fell,
who merely hung on. The morning drills
secretly, like an element that absorbs.

We are right back where we were
before the world turned over,
the dreary steeples of Fermanagh and Tyrone
are all that Sunday means. Their North
was not 'The North that never was'.

Artemis, protector of virgins, shovels up
fresh pain with the newly-wed
long-stemmed roses, pressing two worlds
like a wedding kiss upon another Margaret:
lip-Irish and an old family ring.

It's like asking for grey
when that colour is not recognised,
or changes colour from friend to friend.
I track the muse through subwoods, curse
the roads, but cannot write the kiss.

Birthday Composition of Horses

The country flattens, falling arms first
through a window. The train bends,
narrowing away to the middle,
to embrace a wider Ireland.

In tents on ground adjoining churches,
people floating or stumbling in fancy dress
might be said to have been put through
a sieve, to go home and be nowhere.

Their fingers stretched out behind them
to the bloated banner on top of the main
tower, a black parting delving the fountain
of fresh beech leaves, a cactus about to bloom.

The Chimney Boys

It is late earlier. The faded biscuit-pink
of the infill building inflames the edge
of the slanted blue and white chessboard.

Those darling policemen, we thought,
but no, they really were insurgents,
a swatch of crumbs of colour going dark.

Every room has a soul if it can be prised
open, a little shy of its own beauty,
under the feudal right of introspecting houses.

But those who saw them skylarking
in the gutters, looking clean and wholesome,
were unable to find any text to discredit it.

Factory children, valued as little as rabbits,
or decaying birds transfixed on a dog-spear,
small gentry, urchins in dreary gambols,

they were climbing boys, boys of the best size,
little boys for soot-caked flues,
seeds of sleep harvesting the dew

on what was left of Saturday, for an ideal
Sabbath. A pewful of children throbbing
for liberty, a bundle of jointed sticks,

lashed from their beds clutching their clothes
over their arms by loving Sabbatarian
engines purifying their manhood.

A boy is hard to quench, mingled
too much with bitter wood; but what is a toasted
child, lying in his negritude,
his corkscrew motion, his sable consolation,
to a deranged dinner party? Murder by proxy,
a melancholy but imperious necessity.

Four assorted clergy, bigot and crank,
with scriptural thrust and parry ready
to add their own enemies to theirs,

pin the bosoms of their lutestring shirts
back, as if they had saved as many
lives as Marconi, normal persons,

six-pounders spraying glass marbles
and clay balls. Soon there would be brooches
for sale with 'God over, curse Great Britain'.

Then the vulture, emblem of time,
calling the hour by another name,
will lay sunflowers at their feet on the longest day.

Filming the Famine

1

My meal of pleasure crisped like a wave
in the perfect circle of his lips,
not helped by the winds and the air:

the primal garment of his skin,
and the brush-braid on the hem of his voice,
was an answer as soft as the question.

It was an evening made of cold clouds
and the necessary flight of natural sleep,
which takes the malice of memory into the half-world.

Springs that had carried the steely dusk
only hours old into my heart
lost their coral heartbeat and were still.

The island glittered like some silver and crimson
winter fruit. The river's small leaden blue
pulse was only sad as one is in a dream.

Its whistled lament took blood from cattle
and brought down birds – its scarlet cross-stitch
roped me into grudging prayer. . . .

2

The image of peace was superimposed
on a sea composed of fragments,
fairground notes like a fragile line of surf
came from the stamens of her pearly fingers,
out of the shelter of her veil,
into the shadow of her arms.
She was all stranger, like some war
that had escaped out of a book,
all but Irish, fought according
to the code of the angels.

Mass paths and other useless roads,
devastated by street battles,
and soldiers impersonating soldiers
overlapped in a film presentation
of an island that had lived through
two famines, and still comes into my dreams.

Brickmakers and coal-heavers
and people without end
slid together in a cell of false time,
a summer of sorrow,
flat lines of darker black
in the sunken inkpots
of the brig Eliza Ann,
The Intrepid, the ship Carrick,
Hebron, Erin's Queen, Syrius,
Virginius, The Sisters,
Elizabeth and Sarah.

The springing forms of her hands
were a merciless screen against sight:
but if the notes were high and opened heaven –
they might suddenly hear something.

Turning the Sleep Spindle

Druidic wind, running without a sweatband,
your womblessness sows its white smile
near my face: I use your linen lords' antlers
with you against a wall in June light,
waiting to be shot or lamed or nailed
up like a jackdaw on a barn-door.

Rosette-formed T-cells in my blood
drink the threefold scent of live and dying roses:
when the bull-sleep of a man who has been 'out',
or a boytroop of three brothers, begetting
the same child, breaks like a nut
my shabby, wing-sleeved peace, the only stirrup-cup

bids from a birth-ladle so big,
Setanta and Scathach
could have lain together in its praise.

Blood-Words

Your silk-dry
mate cry
is a name I would cord
to my tongue,
eye-locked
in an eyelet
where the abrupt knot
of your bloodline
touches the bed-edge shore.

The greenest journey
is a torrent
of oxygen,
acres of water
eagle your arms
from scuffing the slim
room of death
to the self-told
faces from two lifetimes.

The Walking of the Land

'Macha was not a Celtic queen but an older goddess.' – Estyn Evans

The date was three years, three months, and three days
before my time (I shall never have a time),
but I have had the frailty of him in me.
He will want to know I am gone.

It was death that led us back through time,
inflecting the deep order with its surprise:
now he can go on further, clean as a flower,
leaving it word for word thought-true.

Because true to his own deepest need,
though it was an assisted death he dreamed
outwards, on gale days and days
of the dead, for one hour only,

(it cannot be loaned). He was bedded
on winter-brown leaves with a sand-filled pillow,
where the leaf-fodder of his headstreams'
first inpouring moistened the rose-boughs

carrying sunshine in their cooling arms.
A fluttering of spring-sown blood-red
forced the main stem of the thorn
through eight petals within eight petals

to the honey that never sleeps.
In a half-conquest, the 'venerable natives'
take native wives, each is drawn to the woman
by only the sail-hung half of himself;

and the ring he wears is square
with a pyramid brocaded
with a double-armed cross, like an empty
sepulchre visited by adorant youths

from which the sky-living untruth went out
to the tide-water towns, the tenders of blue
apples, the white necked church still
curved in the shape of his sky-alone neck.

Operation Market Garden

Soldier father, the death of your mother
unites us. An underwater chain
is stretched between us.
You are squarely in the light,
encased in a tarnished
brass scabbard.
More than once I kiss
your military moustache,
the lived-in house of you.
My quick, shaky kisses
are a preparation of poppy,
or aconite, to allay
your crucifixion.
They are metal scraping
against metal,
as though a whole army were below.

I sign my name all over
your plaster of Paris,
swan-feathers tell of our morning,
I dwell on the sound it made.
You drew hard
on your cigarette, taking
deep yoga breaths,
your back turned
to a boat-cloak,
your oyster-satin eyes played
unshed, breast stroke movements.

You live off the smell of an oil-rag,
but green ferns were striking
out of your stone thought.
A tree grew from the centre
of a fireplace with rotting
brocade bell-pulls,
frozen pipes wept a choice
of salt or fresh water.

Ring Size M½

Two men held a house, not seven minutes walk:
they were more than forty-eight hours free.
Were they drilling with dummy rifles when he
dashed softly upstairs, with the safety catch off?

I was in a horsebox to begin with,
putting nothing into nothing, the opposite
of playing games. I allowed his hand
its perfect navigation, its increasing warmth,

and laid his shooting hand beside
the slight change in weight we found
in all the cash, stamps and postal orders
running through the letters like a naked sword.

Antebellum Backlash

What happened in fact to the people,
the completely blended, pampered, oppressed,
was like a man bound to a woman
by colour's voice alone, by her mock-orange scent
dragging his half-body like a heart
attempting to leave its chest.

The suckling movements of old burns
wore away the collar above the crest
of bone. She stroked his head into her
normal contours, covered his lips' colder continent
with the silvery blackness of her hand,
slept with his hands about her head.

Mouth against time, his foreign mouth
reached out to the edges of her thirstless tongue,
breaking into the woman's already pushing body,
pointing it backward with its rays.
The sound in his throat so brown and radiant
caused her own to not-quite-freely close.

A people-covered cloud that had lain
on rags a very long while, held the black
kiss all the way, inhabited all the open mouths.
Was her father anywhere near,
in his diet of bright submission, that fled-from
daughterly direction of prayer?

The Fissure of Sylvius

On the sun's hooked cross a cloud of witnesses
begin to hang glassy beige curtains.
Skywarm roads mix obsessions and withholdings
like a marriage of already lived years.
And birds perch the way unloaded furniture
seems bound to its shining doors and floors.

The eleven o'clock news with a mind
too newly born tells you what the seven
with its arithmetic told you. In the end
perhaps a flow of unsupported brightness
is more painful than a circle, but love is
more or less additional, if found
not under the first ice, but the second.

The Modern Proserpine

Eight days out. She was disguising
the awful plunges, singing ballads
to herself at night to retain
a maudlin cartoon of her cell.

Little shattered the sea-peace
but a rifle bird with a velvet throat
who journeyed around her body
strangely comforted by her cries.

He talked jellyfish and studied
a bee's muscles, surveying the British
rivers from the weather-side
of the deck. She wanted

to snatch him from his age,
which was young by island time,
like a ticket-of-leave
or leg-iron man in an iron collar,

a mask of tin padlocked
from behind. Such a mere dewdrop
of a mind, his run-off water
would be semifluid by the next morning.

There he was, policing the little
England of the safer north,
erasing his person with fresh
filamentous corpses,

not fish for they had no heart
to scythe. It was filigree work
to prise open his notochord
with her human jaw bracelet

and her necklace of human
vertebrae that was nothing more
than bits of her. An armlet of hair
was one of the main chains.

She coined him like a word
in the clean-cut sinuous V
of her primal white *visite*
with its uppity palm pattern.

All the guests were skeletons
when she dined ashore with ambassadors,
and all the trees were the same height
as his five-inch vivid blue float.

The Half-Marriage

Everyone had returned,
yet no one had returned.
The leather band around his head-wound
would catch fire in front of you,
beside you, to your sides,
from hospital to hospital
like love turned inward.

His unwon war was over
while the war still raged,
its floral surge short as summer
in an amber-brown dress.

In the damp, mulberry air,
in the punitive darkness,
they were like two mountaineers
cruelly roped together,
who abused the closeness
by means of blue, the starpoint
of his eyes already lived by you.

To Such a Hermes

I am the nearly same
lower form of man, my name
will be of no use to you.
You know the sound,
uttered in one breath.

On your land and under your skin
I keep my life, my rhythm
reverberates with the war,
dying as fast as ever
it can die.

My eyes were your slaves,
a piece of waste, a theft,
your wife as it were,
with and against, further,
through, beneath or beyond
this not-yet-a-place,
this no-ground.

I loosen your language
from myself, an enemy
of meaning comes near,
salving my height of bloodshed
with this fatherless spring
the birds I mean
will never see again.

Blue Kasina

1

You walk as if you are kissing the earth,
(she is breathing – why not me?),
or tapping a page like a drum, you invite
the bell of my hardly used breasts to sound.

My second breast imbibes your graces,
the mind-river of my very first love,
which lets the leaves pass through
as when he wanted my face to be more stricken.

You march your breastless body
back and forth with all its volumes
like a frontier, still agitated
by piety, blood beneath your everyday verdure:

as the semi-divine womb is able
to move around in search of moisture,
and will find it in an opening between two arms,
a path slit as if for letters.

2

I am sight-singing you, music
made out of music, listening to the unfamiliar
mass of your male womb and robust hymen,
your someoneness, paid not to undress.

I am just this much inside your breath
all by itself where you die into
the tide of each unique breath
as the full language watering your mouth

with flow lines of water, their colourlessness
almost intense. The drop of my dress
into the pool of my dress is a brown garland,
a fresh crown, that has never been so closed before.

And for seventeen minutes I brighten
by watching like rarely observable
starsets how your thoughts end,
greeting your rust in whatever rings and shines.

3

The glassed subconscious of the city
is overwhelmingly sweetened, the narrowness
of the light is false, the shadows false,
draping the window cushions with gold watches.

So now each soldier has swallowed a draught
of *eau-de-vie* in which the flag's
ashes have been dissolved, we can
begin again with the 'A' names

in the wood-book, using the soot of wood.
It is a kind of confusion of faithfulness,
this unkind holding of the torch of wishlessness,
that turns gently within my unmet gaze

an afterkey not turned far enough
to snag and soften all about it
the regrowth of the cleared table
whose threading would give, mile by mile.

The Language Renters

The kinship of your Shrovetide sleep
is an illness caused by music.
Word-of-mouth news lowers itself
from the windharp of your eyes,

pours itself along the floor
like a day of religious humiliation,
cutting down a road
where there was no hill,

building a bridge
where there was no water.
Our roof tree found tangled
east of the river's law

in a place of non-wounding
rolled one-quarter of your body
a lilac-edged diagonal away
where the black of the current has not run clear.

Black Magnificat

for Neil Jordan and Patrick McCabe

Our voices mild and moist,
baptized with dark water.
The mobile stroking hand
soaking my shoulder.

A rain-affected
smooth execution,
sure to be too light,
a mere film.

Forcing out the real name
of the hardest-worked river
beyond the bounds of the city
and the neglected old fields.

I cup one hand over my eyes
stiff with many inner deaths,
and in a crush of images
with a kissing sound at the ear

appears the moon like a beheading
block, its moon volume
only half-born, a surliness
beating in and between

like a jealousy or soreness
whose warmth never closes –
opened, but not broken open.
You flower her, create

new spotless local inhabitants
for this harrowed moon
whose power hovers on a ribbon,
but it will not be the same Paradise.

Soliloquy to a Cloud

Seven steps from a certain stone
Cuchulain left the track of his hand
in the rock like an unclear telegram.

Where his footprint marked the stone
it looked as if the sea had run through it,
and if you touched it your hands
would come out clean.

It drew me in like a map or sea-shore
pond, or some corrosive blood
demanding birth.

I walked around it as around a room
of sixty candles, lit in a space,
though I do not believe that in this place
any wish was being spoken.

Because from the very beginning all
was lost, all we learned was the art
of letting something die away, never to resume
unended dreams, the way a woman contemplates
her ring as something done to her.

Hand over hand she loops her hair
below each ear, searching the desiccated
womb of the piano for a mouthful of sounds.

I have already dreamed this several times,
an old dream, a stone you'd use for a hearth,
or bridging a stream.

A chamber opens and heightens
as a letter grows and grows.
Within the enlarged hollow
are the seeds of an all-but-angry-mood,
as if rain were on its way, or the river
widened at the turn the music has taken.

And suddenly I could not find the word
for 'death': the motto for this Christmas
became 'Farewell, over-tired year,
I am looking into a purer air.'

(The carpet discharged a torrent
of beauty; a root shattered its earthen
vessel; the lily-seeded dress
grew cosmetic flowers.)

They said that if you threw a stone
from under your left foot,
the island you saw coming up the lough
would stay forever above sea-level.

Only, the two stones are leaning together
like a pair of tongs, the second Tuesday
in May against the second in November,
a town of sixteen back-to-back houses.

And the low red light of the moon
is a marriageable face worrying all Antrim
like a railed grave plot, a sister grave.

Severed tribe, outworkings,
Cromwell believed we were all interconnected
by caves. But night, the doorstone,
took its revenge, and I dreamed
of a path that grows ever narrower,
under the hired sky remaining true to us.

To Make Two Bridges Necessary

The sky is all fresh horses and unusual tidiness;
jets of yellow and lavender marriages;
with a twist of pink silk where its empire runs down –
all brilliance, all morality, all tarry browns.

Now its flecked beige vault holds a seagull
ready to leave like a hatchet beside a bed,
a pencil scratch folded from the day before,
open, with the lean colour of our sleeping last night.

I already wear all that you have imagined:
your knee arched like a blizzard anchoring my chest,
or a swollen river bridge conveniently looping
into its street clothes, out from music again.

The sand between tides will thank you for fielding
freedom with the quick of your hand and the crux
of your ear: that memory-plus-moisture in the air:
more unawakened, fireless lips, unlevied hair.

The Muse-Hater's Small Green Passion

Since that trim February,
enough connected days
went aloud in a letter
a long way round
to awaken your nightside image,

as centuries take a while
to disappear,
as a blessed century
smoothes out in a matching fabric
after the march of words
and corridors of how long.

A differentness has begun
like the growth of grass, hair-thin
in spear-feet, the sword-lily
after the lack of irises.

More slowly than the eye passes,
leaving us with too much
for the journey, the square miles
of suffering shape the bed,
the house, the book, into
the laziness applied to fields.

So we can travel across ourselves
in tidy months
mobile as a language
from the well-knownness
of your lighted parts
and lightless state of mind,

even on the jade of Death
with goblet and bridle,
to the well-marked bone
at the root of your breast
that promised to be a woman;

to the hinged opening
and secluded swannery
of the wood-carved, never-
satisfied manliness
of your inner wall.

Even in tragedy, they were such risks
to my deadness, the angel ceasing
to be an angel, this sharpness
and stretch of pure profile wings
like a downpour of stars.

Round Square

Unblemished by Irishness,
though parted from England,
the light spreads its lesser beauty
like the beginnings of breasts. . .

the grass at dawn is green
as pillar boxes in Cambridge,
enjoying rain after the peacefulness
of being at war. Wasted
by our violence, it never had
the chance to wither.

Confused months locked
into a diary: the house mocked
by a bird-footstep pattern
beautifully frozen in a circle
of wheel-shapes. . .

my sugarscoop bonnet, with its
distinctive blue, my paler dress,
my female bicycle with its
basket of books, its traveller's
Italian

find this other air heavy,
its stars mean as old love
that goes on dying
because no one is looking at it.

Yet I half-face the knowledge
of your completely married kiss,
kiss growing up with air between,
naked kiss that did not,
chilly kiss more than prison
which is going to be your child.

The Soldiers of Year II

A few ladies drumming their heels
sit facing the door, like a groom
who carries a weapon. The flag is there
no less for its ended blue
than the star-leavened blue for its flag.

In the stray sunshine the uncensored trees
plunge their roots to earthbound solace.
Clad in air, the ring on your foot
stands a glass theme in my being:

a stained-glass window half-melted
in fire. I struggle to prolong
its death agony, my birth-language,
that sees in armour the perfect layette.

Like black curtains closely drawn
smoothly along a dark green hedge,
eternity withdraws from the world
in which letters are closed and delivered,

the poisoned oysters of your cloven lips
versifying the 'Imitation of Christ',
the family unlikeness of your eyelids
descending curtainwise the grasshopper sky.

Safe House

I stopped on the lip
of the peace that had no beginning.

In a pattern of soaring green grasses
on the most ascended hills,
I saw three early nesters in succession,
mallards, birds of Mary,
sons of rock.

My skin hunger answered
as the spousified child
holding unbroken bread close
to the mouth, being stayed
in its downwardness.

Here our hill names
and our true lips
triangulated black sparkles

frozen in the long shoulder
of this low house,
this old mine counting house
with its ladder stair.

The Starling House

Sleeping, covered with dew,
the unknown north moves more and more gently,
slow as a woman, feeling its way by arm-girths.

Its rivers grow cloudy, the pores of its woods
do not give out any red lighthouse fragrance.

People step like cats among the wind-fallen
branches, where the rain has vanished,
as if they have just moulted –
as if they have come to buy them.

There is Mr. Countryless, and surname
'Don't Remember', whose number forms part
of his surname – arms held
along the seams of his trousers.

The cloudberries imprison his laughter,
and put a real name to the brown-brimmed colour
of Mrs. Convict, Mrs. Neverwell, floating
like flags of departure
over perfectly white police stations.

Only birds of passage know where it ends,
this enigmatic pathway, or the purpose
of this winter road to seem a close
resemblance to the deserted sea:
the longer the street, the poorer it will be.

Lorica

Sword-land,
this work of art called 'Ireland',
whose streets were to be
places without masks.

A timeless Irish
delayed the twenty-four hour
military time,

a frantic democracy
turning the whole kingdom
into shire ground.

Voting by the head,
they will have their slavery
doubled, so moral green
the soreness.

Mating with the Well

I am Ireland-blind and stone-lined
and open to the purity of death, I am danced into form
by little crosses sewn on to a shirt,
and the mouth of the other world
holds me in the renewed earth as in a cup or skirt.

When a stone screams, water gives itself
where it has coursed unwordily,
swamping the nothingness of the horizon,
the pooled indentation of your elbow,
your englobed-within-mountain blessed clay.

But the rhythm of war like a corrupt star,
moon-dead, volcanic, others itself,
and does not leave when angered, mother-needs
the picked and leafy daffodil you are.

An Invalid in War

If I could buy a comb and paper kiss from him,
and gaze at it, I would have paid
too much for it.

My heart blends with the birthday screaming,
as if it did not exist,
contented as the incomplete sea.

There is a continual dawning in the afternoon light,
which explains why the deer became so still,
but not why she was restless,
as one about to give birth.

A single nerve in his threadbare eyes
neither awakened nor inflamed
the shut-in-ness of my breast skin:

yet gently as when the grave opens
and sends the redeemed soul to paradise,
the wing strokes of the wild bird

heard overhead by tame birds
of the same kind who live securely
prompt these to beat their married wings –

a dove involving a whole nation,
however often it is sold, deceived,
can never belong to anyone else.

Thinking of the Whole Island

The luminous technique
of every thread spinning out of the city
imprisons this river
in a parachute dress,
horizontal for calm,
ascending for joy.

The binding association
of geometrical constants,
the pure, separated and balanced colours
clothe the colourless space
in the greatest coolness,
give the wild eye in need of colours
every extra second of looking.

On its sensitized surface
the white is a blue, a substantial
blue mist, its blue taste
is a law that has been adhered to
closely, the whole ocean
is the perfect lover, the breath
it required, in that perfect wave.

While the sour blue sky
like an unsilvered mirror
or an abandoned airstrip
performs its precise and overstrict acts
as if the irony of blueness,
such an excessively hostile blue,
could change the problem of velvet
to wool,
        as if the essentially
unRoman flavour of words, their shyness,
then ferocity, could be visited
without love, like a perfect song.

Idée Mère

I want words that don't exist, the ways
of killing are monotonous. On the right kind
of grey day, thousands of male flowers
receive the same shock time after time,
have hardly lost their full green
spectral colour to decayed silver-gold,
their coloured colour to the opposite
of colour, when life gets back its flavour
like the harmony of stamps you put on a letter.

Then there's sky all the time, and in part
of the sky that's not yet dry, the high north
light of a fishbone, sharkspine cloud,
the colour of wine lees, like a ravine cut
by rain, continually devastated and re-occupied.
It's the minute texture of its strange acute
beauty that's so good, that's so Virgo
inter virgines, and lasts till that
long-prepared, perfectly green, close.

A Poem for St. Patrick's Day

Necklace lines cross in a kind of railroad station.
Woods on the lips where skin is thinnest
begin to redden.
February is shot through with autumn
like a piece of tweed,
October has a divine budding voice
coming regularly out of the air.

The fourteen hinged bones in fingers and thumb,
the eight bones of the wrist, the five in the palm,
the twenty-six in the foot, form an embryo of years
in the bowels of winter.

Salvation itself is the sensation of not quite,
the grammar of not, whose return
I should have worn over my heart like health
or a spring overcoat –
whose lostness should have been my uniform,
my language, my unfermented wine.

Love-Spot

The old name of the glen means deep grass
and, passing through well-defended ghost stations,
another near-island in the island-studded river land,
its traffic once so light, is losing its island charm.

It has always been held that there is a gentleness
belonging to the abrupt hill looking down on settled land
and the narrow arms of the lough, an outlier
far removed from towns of consequence.

Music was often heard from it, and untimely deaths
attributed to the kind of spume collected there
and held in the air corridors of its clouds.
Nine countries can be seen from its summit

where the graves of three Danish princesses form
a rushy depression. There is no way to free it
until a key is found in the lake on the top
which is seen only once in seven years.

Although the lake is a holy one,
it is death-reddened, part sweet and part
salt. The way the stones lie on the hill
is a dry waterfall of upturned cars,

an underlip of bronze-coloured glass
watering one face of a garden. My pre-war heart
felt it a sort of duty to visit the hill
once a year, as a former torture-chamber

that the crown offered any bright-countenanced
adventurer for the yearly rent of one red rose.
Sprigs of heather were worn during the fertile
hours on the hill and then discarded like the spring.

The pressure of fingers placed a bracelet
of bilberries as the sweetest food, the first
to scent cold air with flowers on Candlemas
and Lady Day, and the other feasts of Mary.

One side of it is decorated with ribbons
and pieces of cloth, and often it deliberately
opens its autumn shirt to show the love-spot
on its left breast, or its neck, or its hand,

at the base of its cheek, changing its entire
course of well-mannered speech. But more often
it keeps the spot covered by a helmet
or a cap, like tongs across a six-weeks cradle.

Wild, inhospitable, ex-hospital of a mountain,
neither you nor the staggering horse is mortal,
as with no more strength than the froth of the river,
you burn in two and begin to widen the grave.

Nightingale-Nights

No one was at the pier
but the all-severing wave,
that by-play,
those plunges,
the softened white of the moon
was in other places.

I had meant to talk endlessly
with him, and come near him
in words, a little way
up the side of the cup, to
there where we first
talked of war.

My brotherly fears meant
stepping out alone into company,
and expecting to remain alone,
or far off sideways,
between barely and not quite standing,
set asunder by the asides of talk.

If he was there, living,
after a week of the same grim giving,
he could not help but be
the one thing he had denied himself
the right to be – the greatest space
blooming without aim,

a hill-mass which would hold
the snow in big, free hauls,
banished from its kingdom
but facing towards it,
its villages in view
to his eyes of seafarer's blue,

eyes that after a winged glance
reflect the sea or a shell's
embrace. If I could see him
before, with his eyes, he asked
me not to ask, I can't think
what he would ask

my forgiveness for,
such days as do not belong to death,
or to its deathly morning,
the yearly infusions from his rare
and recent hands whose lines
represent transparency:

the precious still life
and rich dream-supper
growing far out of life from within
of the tones of his voice
fastened to a page
in only apparently unanswered letters.

And when I slumbered
with the parklike common
of his poems on my breast,
I never measured the pang there
that makes poetry,
losing a part of my eternity,

seeing the broad completed shelf
of his books like incised
sunflowers on a wooden balcony –
the outer man, his garments
hung up in a row
with no body inside.

A Religion of Writing

The island's lock weakened
as in dreams; the sea beauty
of the air was moved
by warmed music which caused
that question to vanish.

Dreams as common as rain
returning to the outdoors
one whom the earth has reclaimed
in the passage from the name
to the body, the remoteness
of name to meaning.

Despite the thicket, the writing
is set low, half-empty lines
with ivy leaves and fruits
acting as punctuation.
Such unsteady capitals,

the backward S, the L
with its foot slanting sharply
downwards, the B with detached
loops, a G consisting of two opposing
curves, a Q with its extended tail

taken up inside, a long palm-like
Y. There are cuts reinforcing
the heads and the forking
of the uprights, letters of smaller
size placed inside others.
Winged death with two conversing
skeletons, a flame
with no clothing,
a death's head carved
with a human head inside it.

Clara Theme

'There is no Muse outside the soul.' – Hölderlin

It seems un-Christmassy,
a non-singing robin
fasting in a tree-cavity
with its neck drawn in.

His beard has been wound around
with gold thread,
his lungs like the lungs of the sea,
black and set.

An abortive melody
stopped at a moment of its growth,
silk mosquito nets
sailing him into the sea's lap
at horse-flesh speed.

* * * *

He had just discovered,
looking at snow-clad fields
in the sun, how to paint
impalpable white trees of spring

when the edges of the world
became dark before his eyes,
going blind after a walk in the rain;

and his tongue felt lame
as if he had stripped off
his body too soon –

the bird-listener,
picturing his birdsong,
heard the slate-tinged yellow
rhyming with the velvety
lightness of the table

with its trinity of fruit
when he came into song,
like quickborn glass
speckled with gold,

a building bird
suspending woven pouches
from the tips of branches.

* * * *

When such a rock speaks,
the breadth of a road
beaten by travellers
pulls the iron out of it

to carry one fall
of his almost spectral hair –
a rough altar, for this collared prey
of a songster.

Pincushion with Beaded Cross

Today, an air day, I fear
the horizon of the city –
an image worth dying for,
though some people lived
so poetically there. . .

and though I belong so little
to the more present present,
nine years' worth of real silences
lay unheralded
like letters clustered about a date
in a deeper layer of truth.

The blue overran, one pale-blue
cobalt sheet, folded into quarters,
I made my same-day, even one more
letter, my thirty-ninth,
now nameable,

to the friend whose name
does not matter: the one who thinks
music is his own account
of what it is like to be him.
I have been so plagued by music

today, tell me, without music,
through some honest person as an angel,
where the ordinary, not special, dead
slip to, best seen with closed eyes,
when they no longer dream themselves,

but you dream for them;
and, long asleep in Christ,
both push them away
to forget them so completely,
and wake them alive

suspiciously long,
till prayers *for* change
to sacred prayers *to*. Thank you a moment
for what you do and do not tell
me, dying traveller,

wave-scrolled with the moon's help,
by the same turnings and same trees,
a choir of muses pronouncing your name
for its name, miracle leading to
more miracle, and hours which do not flow.

English as a Foreign Language

Skin over the mouth's repeating gold watch:
lame piano with torn-out strings;
the coldest of nature's shutters.

Double darkness of those two minutes
when the girls of the empire service stood
with bowed heads beside their switchboards,
and little leaves of faintly perfumed rice-paper
lifted again in the hush
of the world that mattered.

War washing
through one of the more merciful bays:
cavity modelled as though by the use
of our own coffin-made body; season
richest in impossibilities, room espousing
only the least refrangible, least refracted rays,
unregistered, branded in the cheek,
unravelling in its eye-treated way
the empty sleeves of the day, the khaki
accidents of the sky.

House without chimney or the grasp
of the earth, all stove, all wilderness,
all auscultation and maceration,
centripetal and centrifugal
as sea-robbed land: roped-off chamber
last lain in by Swift in his suit
of Irish poplin, glebely riding
the common strand towards Howth.

Negligent spirit of gravity
savouring like a waste book
the year of her dusk: spider-enchanted
double star above a moon broad;
word-stemmed ditch down in the tillage
statutes as the 'first tram road'.

Hessian, Linen, Silk

Through moments of winter,
through graduations of the shine on raindrops,
we have reached the shortest day.

It cannot be disposed of by a sentence,
by sentence upon sentence,
by sentence opposed to sentence.

I turn the absence of snow
into a nutrient, not so far inside it
I feel the world on his skin.

Kissing his right shoulder,
finger by finger testing, does he love me,
glancing into his eyes across wine.

Nothing moves but the rain,
a downward float into closure,
you could scream, there would still be silence.

Something I don't know how to name
waits as if especially for me
on the journey's black keys.

Photocall

I learned to sing 'The Shadow of His Smile',
swimming through the flooded rooms
of his childhood home. It was the sea
language of a mild, mild day; I discovered
a way of turning from the gold 'C'
on his sweater and eleven new faces
watching only me, listening to only me.

I borrowed his arrogance in the make-up
blood, so when I viewed the rushes
there was a single solid red frame
whose eyes belied the most bellicose
hymn to peace. We were dressed for yachting,
in Scotland doubling for China,
neither of us could feel any pain:

but through seven opening doors, the sun
set between our lips moving towards each other
the way the world might die – our requisite
screen kiss like a two-hour Latin Mass
where he matched lips only with the Italian,
pallbearer, boat-maker, ever acted upon,
flower of a dozen dancing lines.

The Gregory Quarter-Acre Clause

The fourteen-pointed star
bells out in the air
stretching across my mouth.

It is a resonantly English
overking that has almost kissed
away my necked bowl.

Chained to me like a spoon,
my decayed thatch, it is
the island behind my island,
but not a place walked in,
creating an island effect.

Obsolete and tomb-led as
the Boyne, it sucks at my tide
as a vase food, as if the sea flowed
all around, not merely to the east.

I blush blue and exemplary
as it zips down to the river,
and flycatches the road's more
ambiguous edges, pleats the ground
with all the markers of the year
into a half-circle of older silver lamps.

After six hours, breathless as
the equator, the cropmarks rising
from their knees house
her cushion and her looking-glass,
her thimble, smock and ear drops,
her glove and seal and canterbury hair.

Thunder: Perfect Mind

My skin feasts as if fresh from childbirth
between clothing and prayer.
I am still thinking, I can withdraw
with a gentle drawing inward,
what a long way I have come
to meet him half-secretly
in his unfinished house.

It is no easy task
to turn on that shadow,
that ray of darkness with a whistle
so gentle, I say, 'Invite',
but I could say, 'Welcome',
resorting to touching
the objects he touches.

Where will the warmth come from in this,
if we are talking with nothing warmer
than the voice with the darkness
blown away?

He is intact, his house in order,
he gives it a light so far above
the never-goaded, cold part of his mind.

Gander Month

The years that are over
govern his loneliness,
his final berth
made a high sky.

I want you frail
careful people,
gun-conscious, gun-polishing,
gun-displaying,

to understand me wrong:
and the poetry into which
my burned heart
would go for you

to be remembered
only by heart.
I didn't go forward
to the touch

of the rotted rose leaves
cupped among
descending pines,
but how much

my thinking was entangled
in the white jade
of his eyelashes,
the emerald facings

on his dinner jacket,
the slow pull and push
of his deer rifle
turning the whole temple blue.

Fourteenth Century Hours of the Virgin

'Time is the uncorrected error of God's speed.' – Ruskin

One does not want dawn in summer,
weight on lightness in the far-left corner,
putting that binding lip around its border,
with that look of age, wanting the past,
wave without wind, current with no fall,
as small as the mouth which doubts not
to swallow the day. Yesterday becomes
less and less like today, and on the leaf
a green-stained glittering like the fluttering
of recently failed eyes. I have had cloud
ravenous upon me as the mountain
in its wearing away, just before the dazzlement
of the later moonlight, charred as if off
water, corrupted sea-water, or Rhine-foam.
And here beneath my foot, the dream's navel,
a kind of central year holding always
by the heart the closed power of the dust,
the many uses of earth. These remaining places,
how are they to be prepared for us,
the too-travelled path to word-house completeness?

Our Lady's Bedstraw

Mary sweetens it out, it blows
into an Irish half-moon. Like a cross
maltreated on a hill it gives him shelter.

It is the pairing bed of heaven to his soul,
an eye-well which dyes his limbs black,
and holds him honoured in its songless web.

In the border-hours his one-voiced cry
through the hearting rock of the wall
lights a third window trees ache towards.

Making Your Own Eclipse

The word comes from a Greek word
for 'abandonment': we catch an untraceable
fire already kindled in another.

When night falls suddenly
for such a short period
in the clearest skies of the day

as a second darkening,
they could not have known
that what they were seeing was the Moon

acting as a screen.
For blue does not mean
its sensation in us, but the power

in it, the behavior of the aligning
light in the pleasure-journey
of the obedient morning.

Across Ireland the blueness will drop
to temperatures of dusk,
a gentle east wind

will blow birds silent,
and stars along the path
of totality will decorate

the late forenoon.
Bleating flocks and fearful herds
will unexpectedly return to their stables,

and patterns of light and dark
will tremble over the ground.
We will keep looking

at the fleecy space,
you curled up with your head
on my knee, saying, we

have been cheated, the twenty-
four seconds are passing and it
is much worse than we expected.

Then there will be the subtle
tension as the Moon begins
to creep into your face,

the cool band of air
in her shadow racing
about as close as it can,

to plunge into the gold spot
where the magnified Sun
will sail under the same perfect pearl.

Flowers will close their petals
while wildly thrashing magnetic fields
sprout from your surface,

so anyone standing near trees
will see thousands of suns
engulfing hundreds of worlds.

This will not happen again
until the year 2090,
but you must turn your gaze

as soon as the Moon starts to move,
and stand with your back
to the black candle of the Sun

loosing flaming arrows,
like a plastic Christ that hovers
above a wishing-well,

thinking, now it is over,
it was like recovery from a fever
which lasted about as long as is possible,

kneeling and raised as if washed
by the one planet where life is believed
to exist – hold your arms out towards it.

This Ember Week

It was my sunflower lifebelt,
the polished stone from the Bastille walls
I was rumoured to carry
next to my breast;

it was the number of years
I did not want to conceive
in my Carmelite bodice,
peony beads threaded
like a ring of seeds
on the white thread of my rosary.

A rock vibrates so slowly,
resonating with us at all speeds,
my turnover of bone
beaten for its ever-widening light,
flowed through the point of breathlessness
and would have lent patience
to the dead unsprayed in the wheatfield,
their primitive willow spines.

I buried my sins under an elder tree
to lose my burning perfume
beneath horses' swollen heels,
a bird-red wineglass at a time,
rubbing the closed eyelids
of my Christ-consciousness
with rosemary in wine.

The bitter receptors
on my mapped tongue
forgot the pagan name
of the wound-herb in the wound-drink
taken from camp to camp.

But one sinless flower,
a windmill-shaped grave plant
Shakespeare grew in his garden
moon-unfolded,
lavender to crimson,
lavender to white, suffering
night adoration,

a state flower, or a flower
of closeness, that earned its common
name, following the path
of a leaf within an annual leaf,
the lip-herb lining your shoe.

The Change Worshipper

We came to anchor beyond memory,
standing on gradual reddish tiles
flaming back at a low red sun:
if this were indeed a room,
if the universe is paved with it,
all over into gold, the light-sprinkled
hall folded the sky up like a scroll.

Even the window-blind was not
a simple muslin blind, but a painted
fabric roof that permitted twilight
though the sun furnished the day,
with a design of castles, and gateways,
and groves of trees and several peasants
taking a winter-bright walk.

To see his home put before me
was to hold a lighted match
inside my hand, a spray of red
berries in an opal pin in my coat.
My dusk was noonday and the day
without evening, for he was all
daylight and his own repose.

To find him truly at his leisure
within his today, his governing lifetime,
was some living-apart-together
like the boom of a warmed Atlantic
at the very tip of the Bosphorus.
My earth-imbalanced voice
posted a sentry before my lips

that snapped it like a spell
after he had found it,
a world to stretch the remotest
fibres of his senses in,
that could grow without changing,
its virtues wandering alone,
but extending their arms forever.

It was not to get the heavens
into his head I put my questions
to the earth, that has at its heart
a collision. He no longer lays
his ear to the weapon of my lips,
(and he cannot lay his ear to my heart),
but with the lips of the spirit, sparkling, he drinks.

The Fortified Song of Flowers

The eight-day clock moves on
not to be stopped, but our time too
is time – stained with culture,
we cover the winds with art.

The darkness is not purer,
opening its bomb doors
to a carpet of night-offensive bombs
devouring the precious air

from the blast-proof windows.
The sudden linking of a number
of fires is golden-bedded
into the heat of a path

whose sun shall search the grave-hoard.
A bird will swathe its life-warm
head like a blade being bent
till point and hilt must meet.

Or else it is taught by the stars
to cry for the placeless dead,
to cry the name, to call
the buried by their song-cloud names.

Though its cry always travels
against the stream, and few now
seem to be dying, branchless roads
blossoming draped by rainwalls.

Someone loves you with prayers
where a road is paved to church,
the flower of your oft-won mouth, hearing
your name inexplicably called out.

To My Disordered Muse

The wall itself was almost hidden in summer
once the glens were opened, the commonness between us.
But there comes a time in life when the senses
change places, or the brain takes all that the seasons
describe, and cannot wait for the first snowfall.

The divisions of the town passed through his own
body, existing without, and without, and without,
the several cities in one, the bell-tongues and blood-
greased stones, the garden of masts, ships which fill
every inch of the tartan river, its last seaward turn.

As if his scentful heart is squeezed in a vice,
the more it is trodden, the more it will spread,
and its energies bleed a ring of seeds,
I dream that he treads on a lily, and dreams of
geraniums, or larch that grows six times faster than oak.

Light, daylight-white, placed over water
structures the water; looking at the ruby-red
shining of the colour on his body, he didn't
so much as move his eyes one-fortieth
the brightness of a sunny day.

His irises not quite touching the lower lids,
as when we tell our day, or a few of the day's
waves. A moment's pause that soldiers know,
his summer led body slipped into the morning,
and drums were swiftly stripped of their muffling crepe.

His chest on the cross-bar, his belted thighs and ankles,
the leader trimming the tails through his left fist
to soften the leather with his saline sweat,
removing the thick blood that would cushion
the blows, placing the patterns where they wished,

each numbered stroke accompanied by drum-roll
and tap, till the lash fell with the lightness
of a feather, jerking his head, and the hands
and feet of the watchers turned cold
from sucking in the tears if they wept.

It may require a knife-blade, or the wisest
cloud of all in the chiming sky,
to verbally change universe, in a tided town,
and achieve a waking in an hourless house
entered by no road, by a body not your own.

Three Rings, Six Graves

There were three rings melted down into one. There were at least six people in the grave but only two names upon it, that of the owner and his wife.

Josephine wore the ring now, though she was unmarried. My mother had given it to her when my father died. It had been her mother's, and her grandmother's, and her aunt the nun's. Her younger brother Ned had used it for his wedding ring a year after his mother died, and it was the only heirloom of her family's she obtained after he died a year later, his new wife receiving everything else. She had even had to beg this from her, from the body not cold, begrudged with some reluctance. It was something she resented strongly, the house and furniture she had grown up with, its linen and ornaments, all going to the stranger.

I went up to Milltown to look for my grandmother's grave for the first time in thirty odd years. I must have been taken there at some point as a child because I remembered it was over to the right, in a field adjacent to the road. But I could not trace it with my Polish friend the first day, and had to give details to the man at the record office the second day. Even then it was difficult to pinpoint, overshadowed by younger graves. There was a date 1921, the name of my grandfather's brother, Neil Joseph, who had bought the grave for his young wife, who had died in childbirth. There was no indication that the child's body was there, and there was nothing else, though my grandfather, my grandmother, her brother, my uncle Ned, and finally the original owner, my grand uncle himself, had all been buried there over the period of the fifties, sixties and seventies. No one appeared to have visited it all during the troubles, and it was only now when it was relatively safe people were coming back to tend to their relatives.

My aunt told me Neil Joseph had left her his young wife's ring before he died, after all those others, but she felt unworthy, and gave it instead to a friend of his in the nursing home who had looked after him more than anyone.

from Drawing Ballerinas

At Mullaghmore

Earth's memories in the natural dyes
of curtains half-fitted to each other.
There was a deep today
in their different starting-points
as if non-being thought
it had somehow got the better of being.

To love the world of that hour
was to hear the weather forecast
for a day already lived through
siding with the hurricane
whose presence or absence was the same.

The islands hung together
through the tasteless water.
Though something stayed back
and did the telling
every one of us
was the one who remained.

Drawing Ballerinas

We are the focus of storms and scissor-steps.
A young girl that dressed up as a woman
and pulled her gown tight across her breast
now pays men to dance with her, as we would tie
the leaves to the trees and the trees to the forest.

A ringlet of hair tied with black silk
rests in a medallion of white shell, a machine-gun
in its nest, a crease in the middle of a flower.
The hair describes a protecting curve, a repetition
that is a completion, a dip in a mountain.

And the lines' desire is to warp to accommodate
a body, a lost and emptied memory of a lost
body, the virgin mind emptied from or of it,
to discover the architecture of pressed-together
thighs, or lips that half-belong to a face.

The body turns in, restless, on itself, in
a womb of sleep, an image of isolated sleep.
It turns over, reveals opposing versions of itself,
one arm broken abruptly at elbow and wrist,
the other wrenched downwards by the force of the turning.

It settles under its own weight, like some weighty
nude. It flattens to the surface on which it lies,
a series of fluid, looping rhythms, let loose
by one last feeling. As if it had obligingly
arranged its legs, or joined those imprisoning arms.

The oval of the head is a wire folded
in tension to spring back at right angles
across the neck from which it has been lifted.
And what are those unnerving sparks of matter,
the astonishingly open, misaligned eyes?

That suffer like a camera, and fall asleep
a great deal to subdue the disquieting
existence of others – an aerated grey, but
the page stays light, the paper with ease, at ease,
possesses the entirety of the sheets they occupy.

The contours become brittle and start
to fracture, as if the body-burden with
its stripped-down beauty, having rested,
removed her necklace, had put her gown
back on, tied back her hair, resettled her hat.

So that underlaid whiteness is reunified
by light into a breathing white, an undivided
whiteness, a give or take of space
across or within that same whiteness, that
simplest of solutions, the same whiteness everywhere.

This poem was written to commemorate Ann
Frances Owens, schoolfellow and neighbour,
who lost her life in the Abercorn Café explosion,
1972. The French painter, Matisse, when asked
how he managed to survive World War II
artistically, replied that he spent the worst years
'drawing ballerinas'.

The Ballet Called 'Culloden'

It was a painted journey,
their mountains were a week by fast horse.

I bent my body to the climb,
bringing it from its order of march
into its order of battle,

and blew on the slow-matches of my fingers
to give them skill.

My saddle-housing gave off gentle
light across the spine of the moor
where the broad road passed over
the graves caught in its mouth,

each holding aloft a flaming
pine-knot of five bows,
heather, gale, ling, oak and myrtle.

The ground rose at seventy-five
paces to the minute, and a black roof
of hats bared their primrose facings
firing at the words of the psalm.

So the day was conceived in its commonness,
a well-known green, and the answer
to my floral question was allowed
to fall straight down

till the trees that were needed
for other men, or eight-oared boats,
found that flower reeling in his fluted hand.

The Mickey-Mouse Gas Mask

In the country of comparative peace,
conscious of trees, I taste my far-from-clear
citizenship: like continental mourning kept
in an Italian hurtwood marriage chest.

I have never been out in so black a night,
people stood in the roped-off streets
watching the sky. The Clubhouse's pretty double drawing-room
had gone completely flat, its back
as if a giant knife had cut it through.
Huge blocks of stone were thrown up in the air
like cricket balls, furnishings were flung
fifty yards on to the course. Every window
missing, the church had only its spire left.

This war of movement seems to travel
like a reverse letter *L*, the long arm
loaded with Maid-of-Honour cakes. The other
a dog-photographer's water-only meal.

The Orange Island

It was not the fault of the day
that it held objects fiercely
like a rose cast in brick
from a seven-sister rose bush:

the pivot of the summer
was so full of weather,
the curtain of grapes
could barely stretch an octave,
one couldn't count the grapes
on the clear heart of the curtains.

Each storm subsiding
in the gabled looking-glass
spun like a bomb worth
boasting about into unsuspected
freedom.

Every dialect
that danced on his tongue
dissolved her internal dream
of immortality with a kiss.

And part of the prayer was wearing
a green branch like a tinge of sex.
Riverside, near no road, it flecked
and slotted, and felt the handle
turned very softly from the other side.

Butcher's Table

We flew between two sheets of heavenly blue
which crossed the top of the world.
Bank notes fluttered on pavements, and in cool,
arched rooms, eyes matched conversations.

He played me a little sad Chopin, the blue-
out was bright, but the fields were a strange
sour green. At some indefinable signal
a hundred horses moved as one, storks in migration

landed on power cables and burned in blue flames.
Some of the tallest are the shortest now,
the burn cases lie so still, beyond forgiveness,
dark marks show how deep the water rose.

Once again we are alone in the war,
we have torn the skin off rooms like dolls' houses,
we have sown the cemetery with mines, a jigsaw
of bodies mulls the dust. If Overlord has started

you must make the gun part of your arm, squeeze it
like an orange in your palm, write with it as a prayer-
like pencil. But what a little life the dead tanks can take,
as they repair our country, with my gun arm against the door.

The Frost Fair

A sudden sunburst, then a world of torment.

The moon, that connoisseur of death,
slept to a miracle, lilac over black,
and left town early on Saturday.

Small, one-eyed town,
downstairs to her satin-stitch,
to a little fixed pain, a continual
motion of the head. . . .

She is still lying there,
her face covered with newspapers,
eyes, fingers, here, there, everywhere,

and she might think 'I'
as she did now,
pulling out the leaves
from the birch trees of Birkenau,

all over, from top to toe,
from left to right, longitudinally,
perpendicularly, diagonally,
like twenty ounces of blood
from the body of a superior bird

whose shrine is hanging by its heels
from the shaft of a petrol station
where fifteen hostages were painted
all along the iron.

The Colony Room

If you are touching, you are also being touched:
if I place my hands in prayer, palm to palm,
I give your hands new meaning, your left hand calm.

You define my body with the centre of your hand;
I hear through the shingled roof of your skin
your ear-shaped body enter the curved floor-line
of my skin. My hands just skim the cushioned opening,
the glitter of your mouth; all woods, roots and flowers
scent and stretch the map that covers your body.

Less touchable than the birth or continuation
of Ireland, in its railed enclosure, your root-note,
in its sexual climate, your kingdom-come eyes,
year-long, inactive lover, durable as paradise.

Like small shocks in the winter, neck to neck,
the mirrors reflected the coloured ray
the evenings needed most, when the day . . .
asked for night in that mistletoe way.

Condition Three

Dawn, that I always thought of as fixed,
the most closed country, embers more often.
Her brokeress womb mosaics a breadth of dusk,
an overnight autumn.
Some deep, unsweetened, sour-smelling ingredient
elbows out the time-related twittering of birds,
nightcrests, walking against pillows.
So that I miss their never-denied noise,
like the largely unheard sounds of war,
the colour of war, and find myself wishing
I were a weather-whipped rocket,
walking into news of any kind.

An unreal warship sculpts the coast
with its watchful, eloquent English,
its cool, watered path, from a midcentury
midwinter to a clockless marriage summer,
has frozen all time but its own.
It has probably hurt someone I knew,
or there is some hurt beginning to happen,
its slow bleed bringing eyes
down into pages, mouths down
to the onion-thin sheets of paper
butterflied, ebonied by the bombs.
Its aloneness corners on to mine,
is quilted on, like land.
It spreads open my warrened days
by the dayful, all its seamless miles.

I am listening in black and white
to what speaks to me in blue, in that peacock
power of voice, whose vistas furnish the house
till the night, an enchanted day, overwhelms
any man-made light. When there is a distance
to it, or a fast from the incense of talk,
it is wound in other voices, in mouths sewn
in protest, in arms crossed behind necks
and eyes which are almost too calm.

A sudden set of midsentence years
will be served like home hours,
or the last time your bare lips'
uncertain shrines were used.

Angelus Bells and the Light Glinting in Her Hair

A searchlight swung across the lake
like a marriage subject to season.
All the ungrown tissue of its sucking depth,
its sharp green, less and less to be found.

The long narrow lane of his face
filled his turned-up hood, as if
a few jags of unpainted bushes
could become a tempest picture now.

War spirit, mirror in the uniform of a wheel –
let us become strangers again.

The Swan Trap

I wrote to winter to remain
watchful, in second place.
When a word was wanted
I drowned myself in moonlight.

The dazzle-painting of my inner bone
and underskin went on burning.
My wings locked in the rich prolonged
red of the dead water.

But the wing which is the sail
is tamer than it was – slow-flowing
conversation is now as fast as silk:
railroad songs can put back the trains.

Like upright script my neck's outstretched
pillow creases take off into the wind:
like a hint of sea on the air, a gentle blue,
a blue feather pattern quivers

the much-decorated, swiftest part of the river.
And so intensely the proper inhabitants
of the true wild dive together,
their killable gold-plated shoulders

diving deep, into each other's
wilder places, where an ancient enemy
or an evaporating memory
concentrates on a square-lipped

lasting peace, superbly green,
its heart as large as a bull,
its arteries wide enough
for a child to crawl through.

A Perfume Called 'My Own'

When a spider makes the initial move
from one side of a lane to the other
she leaves, but she does not leave.
Her ingrained life erupts within her,
she crawls along the bidden thread
she has created, recluse about town,
holding on to herself like utter fragrance,
like a warm but ordinary woman
whose bones float about her body,
whose clothes just cover her breasts.

How strange it was that you should have been
that person, so near to the earth,
weaving in and out of my life, where everything
was missing, by a hedged path,
where to walk in a wood was to be fired at.
The lost summers continued incognita through
the long emotional autumn tunnels
till January showed no sign of returning,
and September passed to the clear month
of June, merely by changing the ribbon.

The face of morning reflected
in the lid of a piano has a smudged
mouth; the inside of a week
of dark, almost black, daylight
drinks thirstily the bloom from your head
like the snow-clad scent of an orange tree.
In a room full of half-dead flowers and fruit
winter's petal-like discovery is your Napoleonic coat:
whose English is English, whose shoulder blades mean
how the twenty-four hours go round.

A Mantra of Submission

My miniature shore is a lick of gold
iced over as his singing dated head.

From the caged area of the garden,
he murmurs across newlyfound pillows
furring my single hearted arteries.

At midnight like a storm that feels
my presence,
twelve raw Muse-grapes
free me from all the years of blame

of being ill at ease among pacifists,
war-harnessed as a soldier to his voice.

The Miniver

Another black date, black gondolas
absorbing the blue, trying to renew
our appetite for war like half-a-cake
eaten by a catfish, or a coconut
carved into a fool's head.

Even the most war-weary marauders
at the hour the century was born
were timing Christmas by the light
on their swords, galloping in every ceiling
into the ceiling of a cooler sky.

It was the hand of God at its purest
set the weapons cabinet with its fine holes
deep into the English brown and green earth
of the very lagoon, making use of heaven
to bind His blues with His own ultramarine.

And fettered Mars, so women looked away
from him as black stone, the colour of their thoughts,
so wine flowed from the statue
of sleep-inducing Mercury, a whole raft
of meanings on the inside of their lids.

This brittle peace, a palm's breadth in length,
is always morning, has that morning glitter,
gives the ever-narrower interior a feeling
of being outside, lines the walls with leather,
crushes the marble floor with her floss petticoat.

She is hope's brother, though the two people
inside her add up to less than a whole:
she is so placid, clean and fresh,
the rhythms of her warrior father invade other colours
than the lilac of her vase-room flesh.

The Flora of Mercury

In the room there is no Christ,
but the goal of vision where my eyes
wander step by step.
Youthful time has bidden him
though he seems immune to time.
Like sunlight in the leaden
recesses of the city,
his open-sided U
has the principal role.
The blue isosceles of his tactile
glance is a Phoenician ship
that knows the sea's pathways
and has followed the same
and only path from the start.

To study a man from his shadow
is to contemplate him banished
from the earth, each part
of his languid, ivory body
perfect and apart,
equal in its freedom.
The peace-wagers exist
in his copied light, a species
of hired corpses, with immovable
horizons, immured
in their waxen secrets.

His rigid gaze shoots
straight ahead, the central ray
of his eye drains the world.
He arrests the servile orbit
of his look, which ceases to behave
like a hand bruising itself against
the initial and deepest layer
of these peace-war paradoxes.
Silence or indifference,
like a domestic muse,
masks the best of war
in the same fabric that makes
that distant, disembodied cloud;
and all this sky touches is free.

Moonflowers

Your small-paned colander window
no longer fights the many-windowed sunlight.
Autumn's manoeuvres almost detribalized us,
a few bells rang out of tune
in the vote-giving city,
some cheering from recruits who
will never be called upon,
flags hanging flaccid
in the November damp.

Constables had only recently replaced
the old-fashioned watchmen,
but neither peace nor war would satisfy them.
My dream of a month ago
is like iron-collared poured water,
doublearches of water then under snow,
the scene that went before that sleep.

If a final omen were sought
by so mild and open a winter,
the hearse-like clouds
are things which are passing away.
Peace has defeated
the careless arrangement
of his slack hands.

And spring is still awaited
by the ornamental trees in the ossuary,
by the English roses added to our gardens,
by that war-worn figure,
standing in the firelit room,
asking for his wife:

by the moonflowers at the edge of war,
their hardest buds the studs
in our shirts.

Gaeltacht na Fuiseoige

New Year's Day, 1997

Cubes of sky-wielded silence
yellow the light: the light
that would be glad
to bathe itself in you.

When for years I have months,
and my soul chimes
like an inhabited word,
a thinking which sucks

its substance, barer now,
enticing meaning, laying
word against word
like pairs of people,

broods in the wound,
an admitted infection,
the highroad's central
greatest ought.

The title refers to the Irish-
speaking area of the Lapwing,
which was part of the Republican
H-Block in Belfast's Maze Prison.

Red Trial

I wanted to buy a man made from sleep:
an underground man, a new glittering iceberg.
But his perilous eight-ninths was so over-alive,
when I tried to interview the ever-present dead,
I wanted the truth and all I got was his body.

Close-lipped and stern, a mere husk, in convict
clothing; with an air of looking back on a love-
affair; actor with a single line, framing sentences,
sitting tensely forward in a pistol-point of time,
so all you could kiss was his fingertips.

A letter addressed would almost certainly reach
his half-an-hour away, H-for-Henry, Tudor-shaped
end house: whose invisible fourth wall was
the whole world watching – a keyhole to which
an eye of every age was pasted.

The radio, that fair-faced conspirator, purred
with a positive belongingness, whispered
his name in Irish, wished to touch him where
a bill of dark particulars, black with one white
glove, hung like an act in the living-room.

'The defendant must have flown during a redundant
winter, when no planes landed, to a burned-down hotel.'
As if last January were standing floodlit, after
a long detention on mere suspicion, free to be silent,
entitled to a hearing, on an autumn day in court.

While sour soldiers, overgrown boys, met summer
half-way in their fall ensemble. What he had 'done'
had a winter-smell of mice and old wood;
its enormity dazed me like a sunburst, marking
his inmost bloom with a blunt malice

to a pirate flower curiously streaked,
though it is the hand holding it that is cracked
and seamed, by its power to harbour him –
the sea in labour every fifteen minutes
against what it should host, the all-night diver.

Hazel Lavery, The Green Coat, 1926

Agreed image, of your open self, your personhood,
do not put me into a sadness like your own,
though I am using your heated body with its
easy mark of beauty, its narrow grip on a segment
of the abstract world, for some clues.

He has been able to bring your inner sun
to full view, a real heartbeat and a lucid mind
inhabiting a body degrading into matter:
like a rosary made of plum stones, built *en*
colombage, your hospitality towards death

is the light of my own country. The lamp
without oil in your spine a hand-made candle
to light me to bed. Your sense of chastity
starts a shape in me attached to life at all
four corners, saying what your beauty means to you.

A wave heaping itself to feast like a plant
on much of what flames in my eyes, the world
of speech, a world that seems bared of its covering,
and has not a bone in its body. You are walking
within a tulip, and a fire of sea-coal in your house

not yet numbered leaves a blue path through
the warm cinder of your head. You throw a veil
of sinewy deception, of half-grown leaves,
over your eyes, walking up Air Street that moon-
ark body you had so often laid down. . . .

so that the living seem to go to bed
with the dead, most seasonably, a boy hobbles
with a log at his foot to kiss the bell-handle
of your lodgings: his most used words inking
that wintry mantle of aged snow, floating

in the middle of the unstitched page. You have
what used to be called a military bearing,
which is that of a child asleep on a cross,
the whitish patina of verdigris and rose
carmethian that begging soldiers forge

on the eight hanging days, as their ivory ticket
to the damaged sky where heaven tries to see itself.
And it is as though you actually wore armour,
with nineteen horses killed under you, seated upon clouds,
your seas unsailed since his blood fell directly

into the unfixed horizon.

Black Raven on Cream-Coloured Background

'A sparrow hawk proud did hold in wicked jail
Music's sweet chorister, the nightingale. . . .'
                              written for Thomas Weelkes, from Hesiod

I too was sorry that he was not shot,
really not thinking of it as quite possible
either, the rainbow lifted off the ground
and gathered into a turquoise ring –
I'll ground myself in its radiance.

Tired is not what I am, but I think
I really did know him, having seven
years to study him, still, he was different
every day. He was already a generation
old – a generation more, our paths would converge.

But he had to be given up for lost
so we would be a little scared all
the time by the unloved government,
its small excoriations, its semilunar
depressions, its bells tied up and muffled.

And his heartsounds were not among us
for years, in any way the world
knows how to speak, his body and tang
abloom with tapers quenched,
his soft-collared, slightly uncomfortable smile.

Though it would take a ship
to hold all the messages, I only half-read
by hear-say all the other names
of the fields; how finishing his last field,
he then cut all the flowers in bloom

in the school garden. The allied fields
kept tryst with the grass being cut
from under my fingers by bullets.
He had invented a lamp with his last
look at the earth, to send the first leaf on,

walled in by himself, and fit for idling,
fit for restraint in handcuffs, waist belt,
muffs or jacket in splints. They said
the bonniest, most dashing of fighters,
his pistol in the ivy at the back of an old shed.

The Muse takes care of it, deeply recessed,
so primitively crushed: she holds
and freshens in this air of withering sweetness,
close-knit and somewhat stifling, the barest shadow
of its most stately, most mobile mouth.

Monody for Aghas

You won't be a voice to me any more,
the weather of my own creation
repeating the highest possible shared
symptoms of the day. You were born

in a leap year, just as one day
was ending and the next beginning,
in a new time zone where landscape
has become language . . . blue bloom

of the faultless month of May,
with its heart set on conquering
every green glen . . . springtime
in action, springtime unfolding

into words, a literature of spring,
spring in place, time and eternity,
she-bird in its velvet dress
of soft blackbird colour,

maroon seed dashed from the hand.
Let me taste the whole of it,
my favourite tomb, the barbarity
and vividness of the route,

my due feet standing all night
in the sea of your pale goldfish
skin without body, its glimmering
sponged out by a tall white storm:

the red flag could not have made you
less Irish, your once-red lips before
and after folded together and left down
quietly, never to be parted,

that were forced open, strapped open,
by a sort of meal of a fixed gag,
a three-foot tube previously
used on ten others,

dipped in hot water, and withdrawn
and inserted, clogged and withdrawn,
and cleansed . . . your broad heart
became broader as you opened

to the Bridewell and the Curragh,
Mountjoy and Ship Street.
It was fifty hours without
plank bed or covering

while Max Green, Sir Arthur Chance,
Dr. Lowe and the J. P.
almost wept, then attended
a banquet, before you smashed

the cell window for want of air,
and the Sisters of Charity
at the Mater Hospital
painted your mouth with brandy:

like a high-mettled horse,
soothing and coaxing him
with a sieve of provender in one hand
and a bridle in the other,

ready to slip it over his head
while he is snuffling at the food.
Today the fairest wreath is an inscape
mixed of strength and grace –

the ash tree trim above your grave.

Oration

FOR HARPER DANIEL

You, command in the changing light,
are shedding your leaves, the oldest of them,
the oldest disciple: you know our martyrs.

As if one has just smashed something unearned,
everything takes place as if after your death,
the whole sea breaking up that comes each time,

its rhymes buried in folds of meaning
wrenched into a small space, the line engraved
around the mouth between the actor

and the crowd. You, ideal book
that contains the world, you, question
born of unsatisfactory answers

and promise of a new question, not dreamt
upon but excavated, as dying,
the lilac drinks the watching world.

So its after-death is also a before-death
impossible to cross by will or grace.
You shattered, you surrounded by flowers,

that unheard-of number Shakespeare names,
fit unmoored the measure of the sky
not like that lifeless stone the moon,

prisoner of its calling and unflagging charm,
but the Boyne salmon prized in its bend
in water colour, never out of season,

its great eye redemptive in the weight
of its dry lustre. How it returns
hedging to its Virgilian setting,

its motion heavy with rest, and
how I am forced by sound alone to learn
from that afflicting language

with its busy words, never to use
a word that has not first been won,
nor write your name till it becomes the man.

Afterword

The poems in *The Soldiers of Year II* were for the most part submitted by Medbh McGuckian to her American and Irish publishers in 1999, with some poems added over the next two years. In Ireland and the United Kingdom many of the poems in the two parts of this volume – I. "The Palace of Today" and II. "Drawing Ballerinas" – were selected by her Irish publisher to appear in two separate Gallery Press volumes, *The Face of the Earth* (July, 2002) and *Drawing Ballerinas* (2001), respectively.

North American reviewers of McGuckian's poems – poems whose syntax can require simultaneous but divergent readings and in which images can proliferate with startling speed – have for almost two decades considered these traits of her verse exciting points of entry rather than impediments. While the non-Irish reader may not always recognize initially the local and historical contexts of a McGuckian poem, nevertheless it should be noted how favorable have been American reviews, and how engaged have been the readings offered in those reviews, of McGuckian's most recent collection, *Shelmalier* (1998), a volume in which the events of the 1798 Rising are paramount. Recognizing that this important poet has over two decades developed a distinctive North American audience with its own expectations of and experience with her work, the editors of Wake Forest University Press are pleased to offer this edition of the poems that emerged from a particularly productive period in the poet's career during what is hoped will one day prove to be a turning point in the history of Ireland.

In *The Soldiers of Year II* Ireland's past remains present: the Famine and its epidemics, 1916 and its aftermath, all appear alongside happenings in Hollywood and in Ulster during the last half of the twentieth-century. Throughout the volume the poet is concerned with the difficult necessity of representing fairly contemporary events whose consequences offer multiple trajectories not only into the future but also into the past. Exploring how poetry relates to such acts of representation as photography, filmmaking, and even radiography that render intimately the body's anguish and ecstasy, McGuckian shows how in those acts time itself is made visible, audible, even palpable. In such poems as "Filming the Famine" everyday events and things simultaneously acquire a dreamlike, uncanny, even timeless quality as time itself seems to move on multiple tracks.

The first section of the volume opens with "The Palace of Today" and "Speranza," poems that, alluding to Oscar Wilde and his mother, introduce the motive that unites this volume. No longer choosing between either the secret, unexamined, sometimes unconscious interiors of a sexualized and often female self (see *Marconi's Cottage*, Wake Forest 1991) or the public, historical heroes that are invited into that self as she did in *Shelmalier*, McGuckian now dwells more disturbingly in these poems at the very intersections of power with the bodies that record its mandates. Skeptical in particular of the command of peace, these poems look closely at those who are victims or beneficiaries of change during an uncertain, transitional period. More often than not, in *The Soldiers of Year II* the body becomes collective, a heterogeneous community glued together by a shared suffering but also by a shared hope. Indeed, one of the most compelling images offered in this volume describes the emergence of such a collective body:

> While I wander about in search of the dead,
> all I see are the living,
> being pulled into full existence,
> emerging as if from a cellar.　　("Life as a Literary Convict")

Particularly disturbing are the poem's two final stanzas, in which a "normal" family life that has resumed after the live burial of war seems as artificial as a photograph or mechanical bird: "Fresh families pose like birds/in the wound-up spring, healing/at a distance in a slower time." Nature in its conventional, temporal form ("spring") here is displaced in two directions: the taut tension of a hopeful present that seems stiffly artificial and, elsewhere ("at a distance" in an unspecified place and time), the realization of hope through an unreproducible, unrepresented, and perhaps unrepresentable "healing," conventionally associated with the pastoral. We are reminded in these startling metamorphoses of a single word ("spring"), and through her natural gift for moving swiftly between artifice and nature and back again, of McGuckian's comments in interviews that she is indebted to Keats. Here, as in Keats's odes, the healing process of the pastoral is forestalled, and the Keatsian pastoral of a slower time – represented by Keats in a Greek object of artifice at once funereal and aesthetic – appears in McGuckian's poem in the stopped time of the family photograph. The poem concludes with these lines:

> He lies in his English envelope
> like the Greek word for Greekness,
> defender of Throne and Altar,
> while the frontier is guarded
> by the small wombs of two chickens.

A live burial equivalent to the earlier "cellar," the English soldier's death is an "envelope," itself troped as a further burial in the envelope of identity ("English," "Greek") and of signification (the "Greek word") until the poem reaches a final image of burial at the border, in not one but two "wombs," two temporal and spatial trajectories. In an earlier McGuckian poem, the passage from political reality to poetic figuration might have seemed easily categorizable as postmodern, and this last line might well have been received as a "feminine," and even feminist, image. Such conclusions could be reached only after hesitation here. Indeed, part of the shock of that closing image lies in the location of the interior organs of reproduction at the public and politicized border, a fecundity whose literal pluralism, whose promise of peaceful cohabitation within the envelope of a multicultural community, seems stark and pointless.

In continuity with *Shelmalier*, included in this new volume are such martyrs as Wilde and the hunger striker Thomas Ashe who died in 1917, killed by brutal force-feeding. But more generally we sense now, in this volume, how art itself may be confining or itself imprisoned, the former characteristic conveyed in images of photography or filming that, whether they represent or fail to represent, lead to a kind of violence ("Life as a Literary Convict," "Filming the Famine," "Black Magnificat"). The latter quality may be witnessed, for example, in the volume's closing poem that has been paired with "The Palace of Today." Titled "Oration," it illustrates a "buried" art (whether acting or writing) in the "folded" or "engraved" lines of an actor's face:

> You, command in the changing light,
> are shedding your leaves, the oldest of them,
> the oldest disciple: you know our martyrs.
>
> As if one has just smashed something unearned,
> everything takes place as if after your death,
> the whole sea breaking up that comes each time,
>
> its rhymes buried in folds of meaning
> wrenched into a small space, the line engraved
> around the mouth between the actor
>
> and the crowd.. . . .

This poem is addressed to the grandson of the actor Gregory Peck, the bodily heir on whose genes are engraved a bodily legacy, who is, like his grandfather, one of Thomas Ashe's descendents. It seems therefore particularly fitting that a child named for the author of a novel (Harper Lee) – a novel that became a film in which the grandfather acted (*To Kill a Mockingbird*) – is the recipient of this poem. "Oration" alludes to how words become bodily and oral, and therefore how words, like the future for which his ancestor Ashe gave his life, must have a human habitation to be realized.

Calling attention to the confining or, perhaps, imprisoned physical rhymes and rhythms of art ("The Palace of Today" begins "The meaning is very much / a rhythmical one, the same law / in blossom. . . ")these poems also offer images from a nature whose rhythms and functions in the present ("today") are disturbed even as they objectify human pain (see the "near steps of unpeeled log" in "The Palace of Today"). Other images of the present moment taken, perhaps, from the news videocam (see "The Chimney Boys" trapped in firebombed dwellings) foreground the violence of what McGuckian calls in one poem the "forced marriage" underway in an island she portrays as still sick with the diseases, bodily and spiritual, of its famine-haunted past. In "Speranza" the renewal of "spring" only "reaches deep into her chest wall," where there are "no unspoken lines" and where disease itself has been represented photographically, through radiography, making nature unnatural: "Lung pictures, white mould on leaves, / fractions of heart, the simpler bacteria / of meaning, slow her breath/to the tenderest of religions." In "Life as a Literary Convict" the poet writes that "Signs of the still recent war/creep among the people like a plague."

While these poems are not overtly militant or nationalist, in poem after poem the enforced forms of peace seem only an inversion of those of the prior war. "Life as a Literary Convict" opens with an image of the artifice of photography (print, silver) and the experience of encountering photojournalism that turns the mind not only into a "weapon" but also into a war-torn plurality, "minds," not "mind:"

> I have experienced a wilderness
> printed black on white.
> Tarnished years of silver fever.
> All my minds are weapons.

Just as violent, though, is the everyday denial of violence, its amnesiac obliterations compared to the assassination or execution:

> Ceilings were lowered and gardens
> obliterated, the deaf and the absent-
> minded were being shot,
> but the clockwork life of the unchanging
> street, and the uninterrupted houses in rows
> neutralised the lava of war
> to a normal part of winter
> at an enormous cost.

More hopefully, the volume ends with the address in "Oration" to a young boy, Harper, who holds the future, who can "fit unmoored the measure of the sky" without, like the moon, becoming "prisoner of its calling." For in these poems persists a promise that has come through in each of McGuckian's recent volumes: while the body may become a shared prison, nevertheless through its agency, through its ability, literally, to *act*, the suffering and even the dead may find, if not release, then at least a common language. Through such acts we are "forced," like the actor and the speaker in "Oration,"

> . . . by sound alone to learn
> from that afflicting language
>
> with its busy words, never to use
> a word that has not first been won,
> nor write your name till it becomes the man.

GUINN BATTEN, *Washington University*